RAIN, SNOW AND ICE

WEATHER REPORT

Ann and Jim Merk

The Rourke Corporation, Inc.
Vero Beach, Florida 32964

PHOTO CREDITS
All photos © Lynn M. Stone

Library of Congress Cataloging-in-Publication Data

Merk, Ann, 1952–
   Rain, snow and ice / by Ann and Jim Merk
     p. cm. — (Weather report)
   Includes index
   ISBN 0-86593-390-1
   1. Rain and rainfall—Juvenile literature. 2. Snow—Juvenile
literature. 3. Ice—Juvenile literature.   [1. Rain and rainfall.
2. Snow. 3. Ice]
I. Merk, Jim, 1952- . II. Title   III. Series: Merk, Ann, 1952- Weather
report.
QC924.7.M47 1994
551.57'7—dc20   94-13325
                                        CIP
Printed in the USA   AC

TABLE OF CONTENTS

RAIN, SNOW AND ICE

The Earth is a watery planet. Water covers about three-quarters of the Earth's surface. More water is in the air. That water, some of which we see as rain, snow and ice, plays a big part in our weather.

Rain and snow fall from clouds. Ice can form from water already on the Earth's surface or fall from clouds.

Water reaches the clouds through a natural process called **evaporation**. Water heated by the sun evaporates. It rises in tiny droplets into the air.

Like great sponges, clouds squeeze out rain and snow

RISING AND FALLING WATER

Water that evaporates becomes **water vapor**. The particles of water in vapor are too small to see, but water vapor is part of the air we breathe.

As air cools, the water in the air **condenses**—the tiny droplets come together. The tiny droplets cling to unseen particles of dust and dirt. Together, these microscopic droplets build clouds.

Water evaporates and forms clouds

PRECIPITATION

When conditions are right, clouds act as if they have been squeezed like giant sponges. Water falls from the clouds. It may be in the form of rain, snow, ice or in some mixture.

Rain, snow and falling ice are types of **precipitation**. Most precipitation begins as snow. Precipitation comes from clouds, and high clouds have temperatures well below freezing (32 degrees Fahrenheit) even in summer.

Swans rest on a fresh blanket of snow

RAIN

As snowflakes fall toward the ground, they can attach to each other and grow. When they fall through warmer layers of air, they melt into raindrops.

Tiny raindrops create wetness in the air called drizzle or mist. Larger raindrops cause showers and downpours.

Acid rain is a mixture of rain and tiny particles of poisons that have **polluted**, or dirtied, the air. Smoke is a common air poison.

Rainy days are for ducks, whose feathers are water-proofed

Clouds cap glaciers in Alaska

Freezing rain turned this weeping willow into an icy "spaghetti" tree

SNOW

Snow begins to form in cold, upper air when water vapor freezes. As it freezes, water vapor makes tiny beads of ice. Beads of ice stick together forming snowflakes.

Snowflakes are like clouds and fingerprints—no two are exactly alike.

Snow falls for short periods in snow showers or flurries. Heavy, windblown snowstorms are called blizzards.

Snow falls on a snoozing wolf

FALLING ICE

Hail and sleet are forms of frozen rain. Hailstones are lumps of ice and snow that grow in tall, cold thunderclouds. Hailstones, which can be as large as baseballs, usually fall during warm months.

Sleet is made up of little pebbles of ice and snow. Sleet forms when raindrops pass through a cold layer of air before they hit ground.

Sometimes rain freezes instantly into ice as it strikes the cold, ground surface. Everything then wears a glassy coat of ice called **glaze**.

A cardinal perches on branches gloved in icy glaze

DEW

Early on a sunny morning dewdrops may glisten like jewels. Dewdrops form at night when air close to the ground rapidly cools.

Because the air is cooler than the ground, the water vapor near the ground condenses. As the water vapor becomes liquid, dewdrops appear.

"Indoor dew" forms on the outside of a glass of cold liquid on a warm day.

Dragonfly wings glisten with dew on an early morning in September

FROST

Frost covers leaves and lawns, windows and woodpiles with an icy, white veil. A crisp, heavy frost looks like it came from a brush dipped in silver-white paint.

When air cools enough to freeze water vapor, the water vapor becomes frost.

In early fall a meadow may sparkle with dew one morning and frost the next.

Frost cloaks young elk and a mountain meadow

GLACIERS

Glaciers are great masses of ice. They are found in the Earth's coldest regions.

Glaciers develop when snowfall builds up over a period of many years, but does not melt very much. The snow gradually turns to ice in the cold temperatures.

Over the centuries a glacier becomes an enormous "river" of ice. As it grows, it can grind out a valley.

Chunks of seaside glaciers fall and become icebergs in the oceans.

Glossary

acid rain (AH sid RAIN) — rain that contains certain poisons from air pollution

condense (KUN dents) — to bring together

evaporation (ee vap or A shun) — the process by which liquid water turns into water vapor

glaze (GLAYZ) — a smooth, glassy surface of ice caused by rain freezing upon contact with cold ground or objects

polluted (puh LOOT ed) — to have been made dirty or poisonous

precipitation (pre sip uh TAY shun) — rain, snow and sleet

water vapor (WAW ter VAY pur) — water that is part of the air; water in its gaseous state

INDEX

Dec 2	DATE DUE		
Kale